# The Seven Sacraments

Baptism
Reconciliation
Eucharist
Confirmation
Matrimony
Anointing of the Sick
Holy Orders

written by Sister Mary Fearon, R.S.M.

God's Gifts Reproducible Activity Series
E.T. NEDDER Publishing

# Notes to Teachers: How to use this book

The purpose of this Sacrament Activity Book is to supplement and reinforce the basic teachings of each Sacrament. Activity Page Masters can be photocopied and distributed to the children, who may write on them and keep them together for reference.

A variety of groups have found these activities useful:
- Sacraments Preparation Groups
- Teachers in the Parochial School [supplement]
- Public School of Religion Programs
- Rite of Christian Initiation of Children Programs

And it is useful in special situations:
- With children who, for one reason or another, have not received some of the Sacraments and need preparation.
- During a Retreat Day
- As part of a Vacation Schools of Religion program.

It is applicable from intermediate through junior high. Encourage children to involve their families, as well as learn the definition of the Sacraments and the Bible quotation in which it is mentioned.

As the teacher, be sure to read each activity in advance so that you may provide all necessary materials and definitions. The activities are more effective when you have thought about strategies for leading discussion before the class period.

**Sister Mary Fearon**, RSM, Sister of Mercy of the Americas, former teacher, DRE, Archdiocesan Religious Education Consultant, and author of numerous catechetical resources, including *Turn to Me: Reconciliation Services, Celebrating the Gift of Jesus, Celebrating the Gift of Forgiveness, Scripture Comes Alive Kit I and II*. Sister Mary Fearon is currently the Director of Ministry of Care at St. Gerald's Parish, Oak Lawn, Illinois.

The author and publisher wish to acknowledge the following:
Kathy Nedder for her constant support.
Sandra Hirstein for her inspiration.
Alison Ahumada and Nora Voutas for their creative illustration.
Aztech Publishing Services, Inc., for their editorial support, design and production of this book.

Additional copies of this publication may be purchased by sending check or money order for $9.95 to: Theological Book Service, P.O. Box 509, Barnhart, MO 63012. Or call toll free 1-888-247-3023. Fax: 1-800-325-9526. E-mail: bookstore@theobooks.org. Be sure to check our Web site for a list of other products: www.nedderpublishing.com.

8 1/2 x 11

Individual copies: $9.95.
Multiple copy discounts available.

ISBN: 1-893757-00-5

## A Sign of God's Love:  Baptism

### Activity 1: Belonging to a Family Tree

When you were born you joined a particular family. You also belong to another family: the Church. Through Baptism you are invited to join the Church family and become a follower of Jesus.

Interview your parents about your baptismal day celebration. Look through your family photo album and find your picture, and any pictures of your Baptism. Share your pictures with the class.

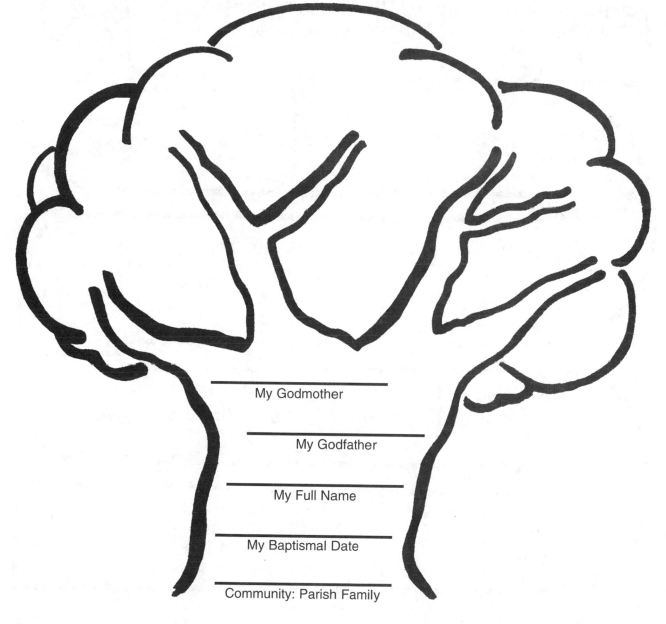

My Godmother

My Godfather

My Full Name

My Baptismal Date

Community: Parish Family

### Memorize:

*Because we are His children, God has sent the spirit of His Son into our hearts.*
—Galatians 4:6

Pray for your family, and give thanks for God's love.

### Activity 2: Jesus' Way

Baptized people follow Jesus' Way. Color all the things you can do that show how you live out your baptism. Put an **X** through the ways you would **not** choose in order to follow Jesus.

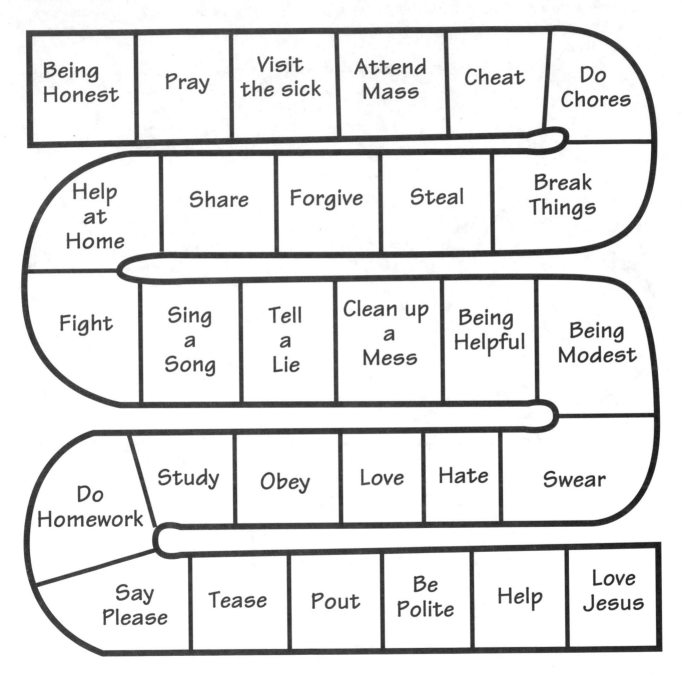

**Memorize:**

*Be imitators of God and follow Jesus' Way of love.*
—Ephesians 5:1–2

### Activity 3

Color in the hand and paste a picture of yourself "in the palm of God's hand." Cut out the hand and paste it on construction paper like a banner. Hang the banner up in your room to remind you of God's love for you.

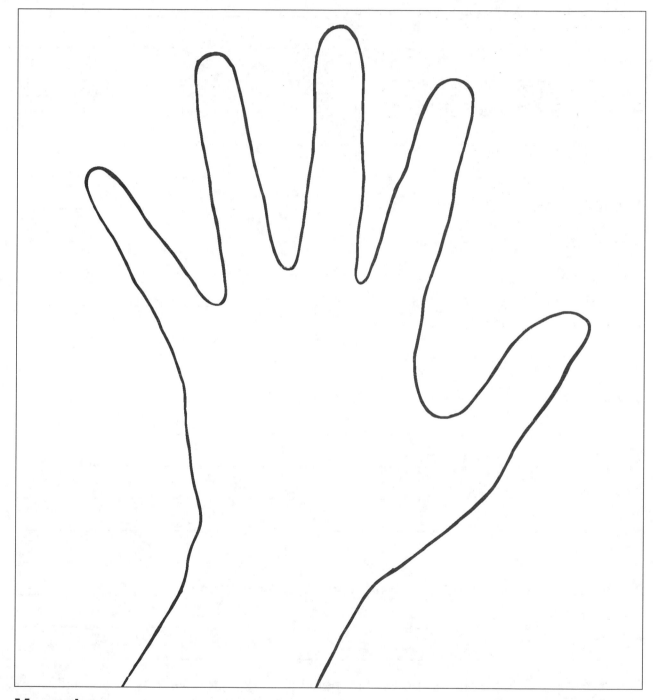

### Memorize:

*I will not forget you … I have held you in the palm of my hand.*
—Isaiah 49:15

## Activity 4

Baptism helps us to follow Jesus' Way of love. We are sent out to share the Good News with all. On the lines below write an example of how you can do good with the help of the Holy Spirit.

**1.** I worship and keep Sunday Holy when I… _____

_____

_____

**2.** I bring happiness to my family when I… _____

_____

_____

**3.** I help the poor and the lonely when I… _____

_____

_____

**4.** I show respect to my parents and teachers when I… _____

_____

_____

**5.** I practice being honest when I… _____

_____

_____

**6.** I care for the earth by… _____

_____

_____

**7.** I am kind and gentle with my friends and classmates when I… _____

_____

_____

**8.** I pray by praising God, asking God for help, and asking forgiveness when I fail.
(Make up a short prayer of thanks for being a child of God through Baptism.)

_____

_____

## Activity 1: Welcome Back

*Prodigal* means wasteful and reckless. *The Prodigal Son* story is based on Luke 15:11–32. It is a story that Jesus told to remind us how a family came together to be one, and a loving father welcomed his wayward son back. Let's act it out. One child will be the narrator, and read what is in bold type. The other children pantomime the actions in parentheses:

---

## The Prodigal Son

---

**There was a family with two sons.**
  (Father and sons come forward.)

**The younger son did whatever he liked. He said, "I would rather not be part of the family."**
  (Younger son steps forward and waves goodbye to his family.)

**But you need money to do what you like. The younger son had a bright idea. He asked his father for half of the family's money.**
  (The father takes out toy money and gives half of it to the son.)

**The he went away to do what he liked with it.**
  (Younger son carries suitcase and goes away.)

**He did not spend the money wisely.**
  (Younger son is in the middle of a circle of children, throwing money away. The children pick up the money and circle around him.)

**Pretty soon the money was all gone. He wondered why nobody liked him anymore.**
  (Younger son pulls out his pockets and shows he has no money left. The children in the circle leave him one by one.)

**There had been no rain all year. The ground dried up and the plants died.**
  (Three children, carrying flowers, hold them up, then slowly bring them down and let them fall on the ground.)

**There was little to eat. The son had to beg. Nobody would even give him a piece of bread.**
  (Younger son kneels down. Another child comes forward gripping a loaf of bread, but will not give any to the kneeling boy.)

**He finally found a job feeding pigs. It was not a pleasant job. He became so hungry that he went after the pig food and ate it.**
  (Younger son carries a bowl, pretending he is eating the pig's food.)

**He said to himself, "I wanted to do what I liked, but now look at me. Is this what I like?" "No," he answered.**
  (Younger son sits down and covers his face and thinks.)

**He said, "I had better go home to my father." And he went home.**
  (Younger son picks up the suitcase and starts home.)

**But his father saw him coming even when he was still far down the road. And the father ran out and kissed his son, because he was so glad to have him back.**
  (Father comes out with outstretched hands and embraces the son.)

**The son was ashamed to be treated like an important part of the family. He stretched his hands up to his father.**
  (Younger son kneels down, but the father makes him stand up.)

His father didn't listen. He was too happy. He sent for the best clothes to dress his younger son in.

(A child carries in the clothes. The father dresses up the younger son.)

The father gave a big welcome party with dancing and lots to eat. He said, "My younger son is part of my family again."

(All children come forward, hold hands in a big circle, then clap to the sound of the music.)

## THE END

---

Answer these questions from the story *The Prodigal Son*:

1. Why did the younger son run away?

_____

2. When he had lots of money and fun, how did he feel?

_____

3. After times got hard and he had nothing, what did he do?

_____

4. Did his father forgive him when he came home to be one with his family?

_____

5. How did the father show his forgiveness?

_____

6. How did the son show his sorrow?

_____

7. Who was this loving father like?

_____

Reconciliation is the sacrament that brings us together again with God, others, and ourselves. Do you know the prayer that shows we are contrite or sorrowful for our selfish actions? Learn how to pray this forgiving prayer:

### The Act of Contrition

O my God, I am sorry for my sins,
in choosing to sin, and failing to do good,
I have sinned against you and your Church.

I firmly intend, with the help of your Son,
to make up for my sins and to love as I should.

## Memorize:

*The Lord is merciful and loving, slow to become angry and full of constant love.*
—Psalms 10

## Activity 2: Today's News

Sins are Selfish Acts that Destroy Peace. Sin is freely choosing to do what is wrong.
What kinds of things do you hear on the T.V. news?
What kind of acts make our world a place of selfishness and dishar-mony? Fill in the T.V. screen to the right with as many words, or draw-ings of incidents that prevent love and peace.

Pretend you are a T.V. announcer, and use the phrase in boldface to report to your classmates about one of the events you put in the screen

**Memorize:**

*If you forgive the faults of others, the Father will forgive you.*
　　　　　　　　　—Matthew 13:15

I am _____ broadcasting from
station _____ about some sad
events that have upset our peace...

I am _____ broadcasting
from station JOY 5. Today a
wonderful thing happened...

We also hear of --heart-warming incidents that help bring peace, here and all over the world. Fill in the T.V. screen to the left with as many positive words or drawings of Good News as you can think of. Again, take time to share the inci-dents with your classmates as a T.V. newcaster. As a group, discuss how we can do away with evil in our world.

**Memorize:**

*Happy are all who hear the Word of God and put it into practice.*
　　　　　　　　　—Luke 11:28

## Activity 1: Prepare for Mass

Set the Altar Table by drawing the following:

- candles at each side of the altar
- a large book on the altar

- a priest at the altar

- people around the altar
- a paten (plate) to hold the host (bread)
- a chalice (cup)

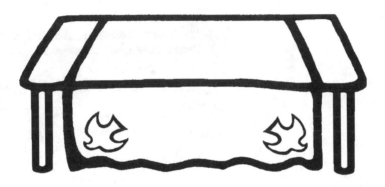

**Christ has died. Christ is risen. Christ will come again.**

## The Words of Consecration

Then our priest says and does what Jesus said and did at the Last Supper.
The Lord Jesus, on the night he was betrayed, took a piece of bread, gave thanks to God, broke it, and said, "This is my body, which is for you. Do this in memory of me." In the same way, after the supper, he took the cup and said, "This cup is God's new covenant, sealed with my blood. Whenever you drink it, do so in memory of me." (I Corinthians 11:23–25)

## Extra Activity:

*Eucharist* means thanksgiving. At home, write a note to Jesus, thanking Him for all He has given us. We show our thanks for all that God has given us through Jesus by saying, "Amen." *Amen* means "yes, I believe."

## Memorize:

*Jesus said, "I am the bread of life. He who comes to me will never be hungry; he who believes in me will never be thirsty."*
—John 6:35

## Activity 2

Color all the even numbers yellow. Color the odd numbers red. Cut out and paste on black construction paper.

The cross reminds us of Jesus' death. The colored design reminds us of Jesus' Resurrection.

## Memorize:

*Christ has died, Christ is risen, Christ will come again.*

 ©E.T. Nedder Publishing

## Activity 3: The Eucharist Celebration
Using words, symbols, and drawings, fill in the empty spaces.

| I. Opening Rites | II. The Liturgy of the Word |
|---|---|
| During the opening, we stand and sing our welcome | God speaks to us through the Bible. We listen to God's Word. |
| **III. The Preparation of Gifts** | **IV. Liturgy of the Eucharist** |
| We bring gifts of bread and wine. In the Eucharistic Prayer, we offer our gifts to God. God the Father changes them and gives them back as Jesus. | In the Eucharistic Prayer, we remember all that God has done for us. Our priest does what Jesus did at the Last Supper. |
| **V. The Words of Consecration** | **VI. The Eucharistic Prayer** |
| He took bread and gave thanks and praise. He broke the bread, gave it to His disciples, and said, "Take this, all of you, and _____ it: this is my body which will be _____ up for you." Now the sacred bread is Jesus.<br><br>Again He gave thanks and praise, gave the cup to His disciples and said, "Take this, all of you, and drink from it: This is the cup of my blood, the blood of the new and everlasting covenant." Now the sacred wine is _____. | We thank God through Jesus for all He has done for us. "Through Him, with Him, in Him, in the unity of the Holy Spirit, all glory and honor is yours, almighty Father, forever and ever." _____. |

**12**

## VII. The Communion Rite

### The Sacred Bread

To receive Jesus in Holy Communion, cup your left hand, and place your right hand under it. The priest will put the host on your hand. Then take the sacred host with your right hand, place it in your mouth, and eat it. You may also receive Communion directly on your tongue. Extend your tongue. The priest will place the host on it for you to eat. The priest says "Body of Christ." You answer "Amen." (Yes, I believe.)

### The Sacred Cup

Take the cup with one hand, while supporting it with the other. Or using both hands, take the cup, bring it to your lips, and take a small drink from it. You also may let the Eucharistic minister hold the cup while you guide it toward your lips. Then take a small drink from the cup. The Eucharistic Minister says "Blood of Christ." You answer "Amen. The bread and wine is truly Jesus."

### Memorize:

*All look to you for food when they hunger; you open your hand, they feast.*
—Psalms 104:27–28

## VIII. The Closing Rites

We praise and bless the Father. We ask Jesus to always be one with us. The priest blesses us and sends us forth to love and serve the Lord.

Tell three ways you can love and serve the Lord:

At Home _____

_____

_____

At School_____

_____

_____

In Your Parish _____

_____

_____

### Memorize:

*You spread a table before me: my cup is more than full.*
—Psalms 23:5

## Activity 1: Choosing Your Saint

I Choose _____ as my Saint.

| | |
|---|---|
| Where my Saint was born.<br>The year he/she was born. | This is what my Saint did that inspires me. |
| This is how I can imitate my Saint.<br>(Write a short prayer.) | I pray to my Saint for courage to always choose to be a follower of Jesus.<br>(Write a short prayer for courage.) |
| This is how my Saint died. | Picture of my Saint<br>(Draw or paste a picture of Saint.) |

## Memorize:

*Bring joy to me, your servant. I offer myself to you.*
—Psalms 86:4

### Activity 2: A Request Letter to the Pastor

Confirmation is the gift of fuller participation in the Church through the power of the Holy Spirit. The Holy Spirit fills us with gifts we need to live our Christian faith. The sacrament of Confirmation enables us to live our faith as true active followers of Jesus. We are to be responsible witnesses to the Good News of Jesus today. In you letter:

I.  Express your desire to receive Confirmation
    a. Include Pastor's name and Parish
    b. Tell when you were baptized
    c. Tell why you are better able to choose your faith now.

II. Think about which Saint you would choose and why
    a. Give the name of the Saint
    b. Tell a little about the Saint
    c. Tell something that inspired you to choose this person.

III. Confirmation prepares us to act in a responsible way
    a. Tell about a service project you will do
    b. Tell about your Sponsor and how that person can help you.

After you type or re-write your request letter, share it with your parents. Have a parent sign the request at the bottom, below your own signature

Choose one reading from each column, circle it and summarize it in the spaces below.

| | | |
|---|---|---|
| **Isaiah 11:1–4** | **Acts 2:1–4** | **Romans 8:14–17** |
| **Isaiah 42:1–3** | **Acts 8:14–17** | **1 Corinthians 12:4–11** |
| **Isaiah 61:1–9** | **Acts 10:37–44** | **Galatians 5:22–26** |
| **Ezekiel 36:24–28** | **Acts 19:1–6** | **Ephesians 1:13–14** |
| **Joel 2:23–30** | | **Ephesians 4:1–3** |

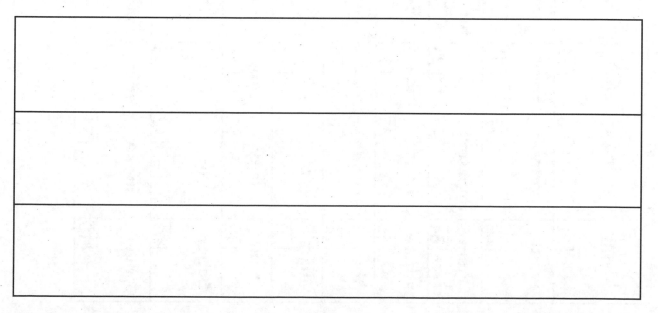

## Activity 3

To read this Bible verse from Acts of the Apostles 2:1–4, read each word in numerical order. Write the Bible verse below the chart.

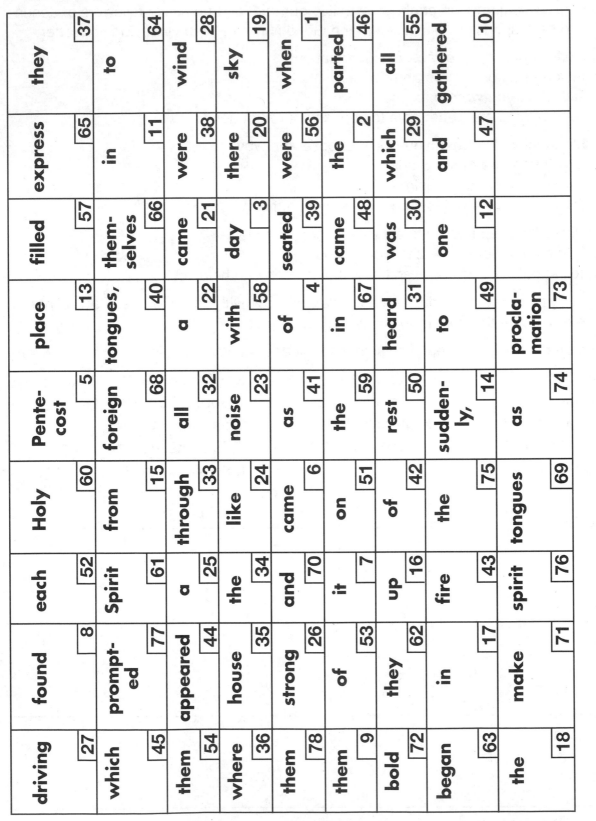

## Activity 4: Gifts of the Holy Spirit

Match the Gift of the Holy Spirit with the definition. Design a stained-glass window and color it in.

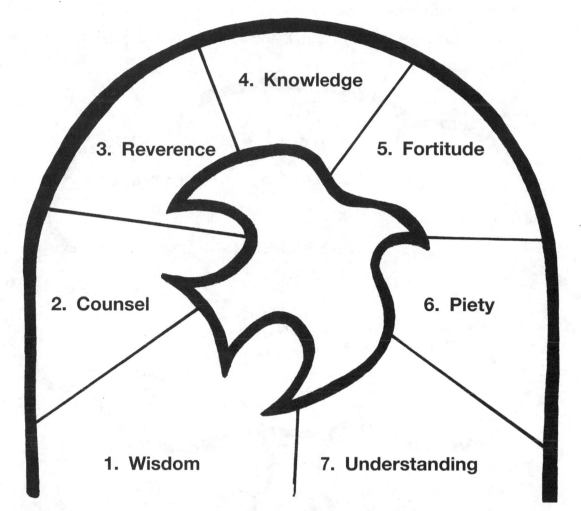

Show respect and reverence for God, God's people, and God's world

_____ Practice with great courage what we believe

_____ Guide others in their faith

_____ Know how to choose the right thing to do

_____ Pass on our faith and know how to make good decisions

_____ Live the Good News willingly and pray for ourselves and all people

_____ Learn about our faith from the Bible and our Catholic Tradition

## Memorize:

*Come, holy Spirit; Shine on us the radiance of your light.*
—Revelations 5:5
*Come Holy Spirit and enkindle in me the fire of thy Divine Love.*
—Revelations 1:5

**17**

## Activity 5: Fruit of the Spirit

The Fruit of the Holy Spirit are the good things that people see in us when we use the Gifts of the Holy Spirit. They are love, joy, peace, patience, kindness, goodness, faithfulness, humility, and self-control.

Circle the words, making the shape of a fruit, and color them. There can be more than one kind of fruit.

What does it mean to have a good spirit? Do you know some groups, families, clubs, or teams that show a good spirit? On the lines below, name the group, and give some examples how they put their goodness (fruit) into action. How can you manifest some of the fruit of the spirit in your family?

_____

_____

_____

_____

_____

### Activity 1: Mandala

God said, "Let us make human beings in our own likeness. Let them rule the fish of the sea, the birds of the air, the cattle, the creeping things, and the wild animals." And so it happened. In God's own likeness God created Man and Woman. God said, "It is very, very good."
—Genesis 1:27 (paraphrased)

Fill in the mandala with creatures that God made. Draw a man and woman inside the heart. Why did God see that it was good for man and woman to love and be in domain over all creatures?

## Activity 2: The Marriage Feast of Cana
Trace over the dotted lines. Color in the jars and draw in the characters.

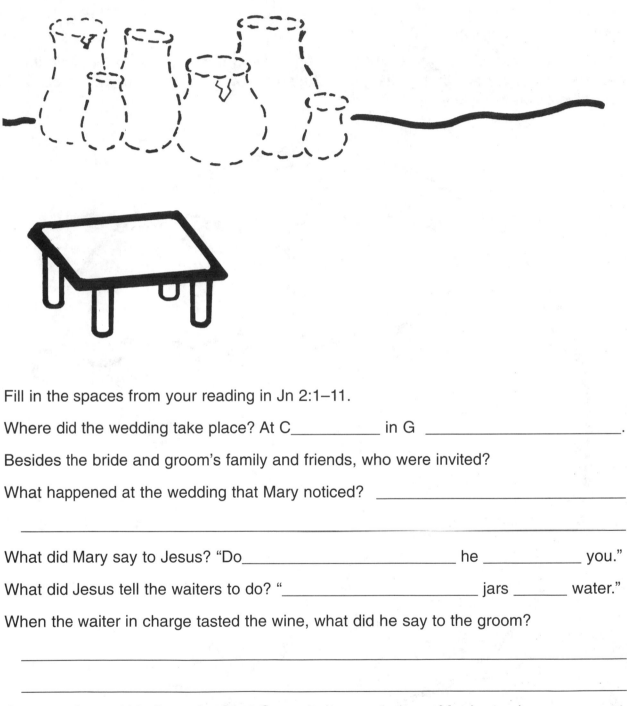

Fill in the spaces from your reading in Jn 2:1–11.

Where did the wedding take place? At C_____ in G _____.

Besides the bride and groom's family and friends, who were invited?

What happened at the wedding that Mary noticed? _____

_____

What did Mary say to Jesus? "Do_____ he _____ you."

What did Jesus tell the waiters to do? "_____ jars _____ water."

When the waiter in charge tasted the wine, what did he say to the groom?

_____

_____

Jesus performed his first miracle at Cana during a marriage. Matrimony is a sacrament by which a baptized man and baptized woman bind themselves for life in marriage and receive the grace to carry out their duties to each other and to their children.

### Activity 3

Discuss the marraige picture.

### Marriage Vows

"I, (name), take you, (Name), to be my wife (or husband). I promise to be true to you in good times and in bad, in sickness and in health. I will love you and honor you all the days of my life."

The Holy Spirit gives the couple the grace to live this sacrament faithfully, and well.

*God is love: let us love one another as He has loved us.*

—I Jn. 4:8–11

*...no one has ever seen God. Yet if we love one another, God dwells in us, and His love is brought to perfection in us.*

—I Jn. 4:7–12

Read and discuss the meaning:
Because of marriage, children come into the world and new families grow and share life. How can families show a special love and care for each other, and show respect for their parents?

_____

_____

_____

_____

## Activity 4

Each of us has a vocation. We are called to serve the Church, the people of God, and to love one another. We can choose now to prepare for the future. A candle reminds us that we should "let our light shine." Sometimes, the couple come forward and light the wick together, showing they will be one in love and service to Christ and others. Color the candle in mosaic fashion, showing ways you can begin now to be a wife or husband, true to one another and the Church.

List some things you can do now that show love and service. How can you be true to one another and to the church. Write some ideas on the candle.

_____

_____

_____

_____

**22**

### Activity 1: Preparation and Caring for Our Sick

Our Priest has the power to anoint those who are very ill or dying. Other members in the Parish have a special call to help and care for the sick and homebound. These ministers are true witnesses to God's love for the poor, lonely, sick, and needy. They prepare the way and involve the whole Church in praying for our sick.

Talk about the characters in the following stories, and explain how the people are doing Christ's Mission on earth. Tell about others you know who help. Tell what you can do.

**Sister Mary Becket** is a nurse. She visits the sick every week and brings Holy Communion. She blesses the person and listens to their needs.

Why is Mary a true Minister of Care? How does she show Christ to others?

_____

**Florence Styx** is mother of ten grown children. She frequently helps out in Church, and drives people who need rides on Sunday. She is a wonderful resource to Sister Mary. She knows where to order the Holy Cards, flowers, and she attends all the meetings.

Why is Florence a witness of God's Loving Mercy?

_____

**Mrs. McGinnis' kindergarten children** make cards for the homebound. At Christmas the cards are attached to the Poinsettia Plants. The homebound read the cards, give broad smiles, and sometimes tears shine in their eyes.

How do the children feel praying for their new friends?

_____

How have Mrs. McGinnis and her class shown love for the homebound?

_____

After the sick come home from the hospital, they call Sister Mary for help or to receive Holy Communion. Sister Mary contacts Ministers who generously give their time. Sometimes, the sick person needs a ride to Sunday Mass and a volunteer drives them.

How does the volunteer comfort the sorrowful?

_____

**Father John White** is an elderly but very enthusiastic priest. He celebrates Mass every month at the nursing home; he hears reconciliation, preaches the Word, and asks questions. He also takes time to anoint all the patients. He radiates joy in his priesthood.

How is Father John White a true disciple and priest of the Lord?

_____

## Activity 2

Look at what is set up on the table for the sick. Anointing can take place at home, in the hospital, or in an emergency or accident. In the latter case, the table is not set.

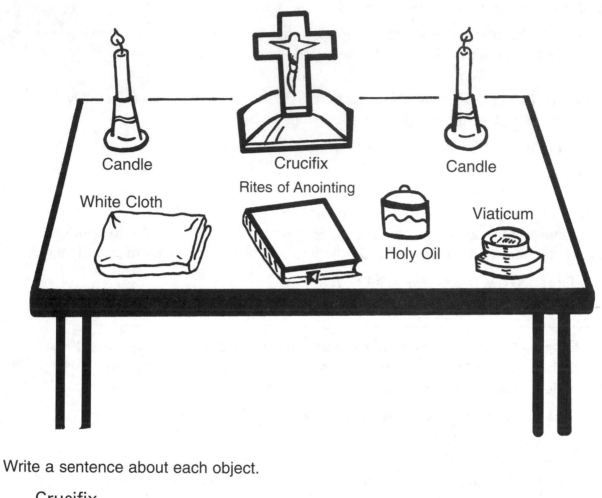

Write a sentence about each object.

Crucifix _____

Candles _____

Rites of Anointing _____

White Cloth _____

Holy Oil _____

Viaticum _____

The sacrament of Anointing also can take place during a Mass. After the Liturgy of the Word, family, friends, and other members of the Parish come together with the sick and elderly. Helpers assist those in wheel chairs or who need help. Often there is a treat after the Mass to celebrate this great sacrament.

## Activity 3

Anointing of the Sick is the Sacrament for the seriously ill, infirm, and aged. The Priest anoints the person with blessed oil, and offers prayers for restoring his or her health. The Church prays, asking God to help the sick with their suffering, to forgive their sins, and to bring them to Jesus, their savior.

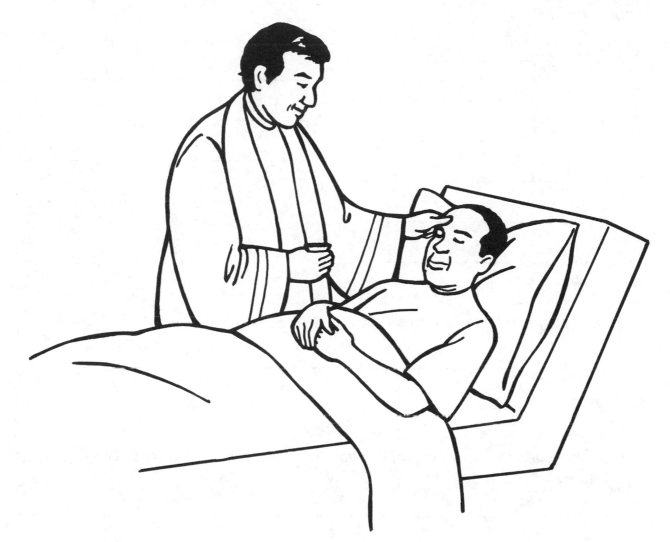

## Procedure for Anointing of the Sick

1. Priest lays hands on the head of the ailing person.

2. He anoints the person's forehead with oil, saying, "Through the holy anointing may the Lord in His love and mercy help you with the grace of the Holy Spirit."

3. He anoints the person's hands, saying, "May the Lord who frees you from sin save you and raise you up."

**Activity 4:**

We do what we can to help our friends and relatives when they are sick. It is also important to respect our own bodies as God intended.

Can you name six ways we can take care of our bodies?

1. _____

2. _____

3. _____

4. _____

5. _____

6. _____

Name five ways we can abuse our bodies.

1. _____

2. _____

3. _____

4. _____

5. _____

Make up a prayer for people who are sick:

For _____

that they may _____ .

How can we support our Church in its effort to do away with disease, poverty, hunger, homelessness, and drugs?

_____

_____

_____

_____

**Extra Activity:**

Choose one way you can help the Church, and make a poster. Label the poster "Make our world a better place."

## A Sign of God's Love:  Holy Orders

### Activity 1

Jesus chose twelve special helpers, called Apostles, to be the first leaders of the Church. They were to carry out Jesus' mission on Earth. Today our priests, deacons, and bishops continue the mission of the Apostles. Circle words and phrases that complete the sentences below.

| | | |
|---|---|---|
| PREACHES | REMEMBRANCE | SACRAMENTS |
| BAPTISM | HOLY ORDERS | APOSTLES |
| FORGIVES | SACRIFICE of the MASS | BISHOPS |
| SINS | EASTER SUNDAY | PRIESTS |
| JESUS | PRIESTHOOD | POWER |
| ANOINTS | | |

1. What did Jesus give to His Church at the Last Supper?
   **S**_____ of the  **M**_____ .

2. Who did He make priests?  **A**_____.

3. The power to offer sacrifice in the name of Jesus and of His Church made the Apostles  **P**_____.

4. Priestly power is passed on to others in the Sacrament of  **H**_____ **O**_____.

5. These  **B**_____ ordained other  **B**_____ and priests.

6. The  **P**_____ of  **P**_____ comes from Jesus.

7. Our priest  **F**_____ **S**_____ in Jesus' name.

8. Jesus said, "Do this in  **R**_____ of Me."

9. Our priest  **A**_____ the sick.

10. Our priests do what  **J**_____ did at the Last Supper.

11. Our priest  **P**_____ God's Word.

12. Our priest administers the  **S**_____.

13. Through  **B**_____ we are called to the priesthood.

14. On  **E**_____ **S**_____ Jesus gave the Apostles power to forgive sins.

### Memorize:

*The spirit of the Lord God is upon me, because the Lord has anointed me; He has sent me to bring glad tidings.*
—Isaiah 61:1

## Activity 2:

Here are some of the ways our priests minister to us. Look at the pictures and identify the sacrament the priest or bishop is performing. How is the bishop/priest serving his people?

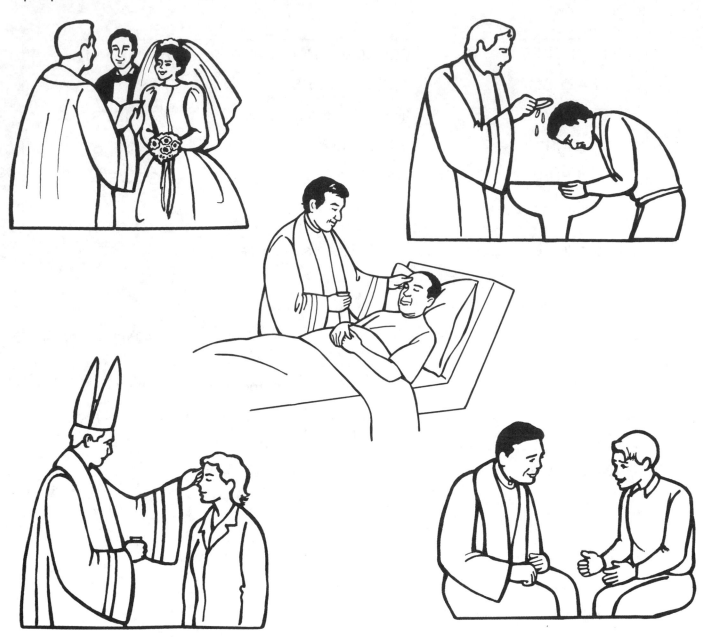

The Sacrament of Holy Orders is a sign through which a man shares in Jesus Christ's priesthood as an ordained bishop, priest, or deacon.

By Baptism each of us is given a share in Jesus Christ's priesthood. We are not ordained, but we are called to preach and teach the Good News. We are called to serve the poor and the needy and bring peace in our families, our parish, and our world. How can you help build God's kingdom of peace on Earth?

©E.T. Nedder Publishing

## Activity 3

**1.** Take time out to interview one of the ministers in your parish.

| THE MINISTRY OF THE . . . | | |
| --- | --- | --- |
| **BISHOP** | **PRIEST** | **DEACON** |
| Who is the present Pope? _____ <br><br> He is the Bishop of Rome, with the Eternal City as his diocese. He is Vicar of Jesus Christ, successor of Peter. He has supreme power over the Universal Church. <br><br> Name the Bishop over your Diocese. _____ <br><br> What are his duties? _____ _____ _____ | Who is the pastor of your parish? _____ <br><br> A Pastor is delegated as pastor of a parish. He rules the parish in his own name, but under the delegated authority of the Bishop. <br><br> Name the priests who serve in your parish. _____ _____ <br><br> A priest is ordained. He teaches, ministers, and governs. | Do you have any deacons in your parish? What are their names? _____ _____ _____ <br><br> What is their role? _____ <br><br> Assisting the celebration of Mass, preaching, administering Holy Communion, and baptism with permission. What other ways do they serve the Church? _____ _____ _____ |

**2.** Write a thank you note to one of your parish priests or deacons.

Read and summarize the following Scripture passages:

| | |
| --- | --- |
| **Psalm 110:4** | |
| **Exodus 19:6** | |
| **2 Timothy 1:6–7** | |
| **Hebrews 7:24** | |
| **I Peter 2:5** | |

Match the Sacrament with its definition:

**1. Baptism**

_____ The Church celebrates Christians' union with Christ and in Christ.

**2. Reconciliation**

_____ The Church celebrates the healing presence of God, who offers strength, hope, and peace to the suffering.

**3. Eucharist**

_____ The Church celebrates the ordination of men who have accepted God's call to be ordained priests.

**4. Confirmation**

_____ The Church celebrates the adding of a new member to the Body of Christ, the Church, in the Trinity.

**5. Matrimony**

_____ The Church celebrates the fullness of membership that the confirmed person enjoys.

**6. Anointing of the Sick**

_____ The Church celebrates the union of a woman and a man who pledge themselves to love one another faithfully and to share their love with their children.

**7. Holy Orders**

_____ The Church celebrates God's forgiveness and the peace it brings to God's People.

Our priests need our love and support. They minister the Sacraments and in this way help us to follow Jesus all the way along our journey of life.

Of all the Church's signs, the most important are the Seven Sacraments:  Baptism, Reconciliation, Eucharist, Confirmation, Matrimony, Anointing of the Sick, and Holy Orders.

They are the Church's most important signs because they call to mind and celebrate God's presence in our lives, and they deepen and strenghten our union with God.

Through the sacraments, God offers us the gift of grace, which is God's own life, the life of the Trinity.

Pray every day that God guides you and helps you to choose the calling where you will love and serve others. In this way you will love yourself and find true happiness.

_One thing I ask of the Lord; this I seek: to dwell in the House of the Lord all the days of my life..._
—Psalms 27:4

## Reconciliation

**Activity 1: Welcome Back**
Discuss the meaning of *Prodigal*. Have materials available: suitcase or bag, toy money, flowers, loaf of bread, bowl, tunic, slippers, and ring. Choose a child for each of the main roles. Involve all the children by inviting those without specific roles to join into the celebration at the end of the story. For the celebration, use a cassette of music that is cheerful and rhythmic enough for the children to clap to. You might want to give them all a light treat.

**Activity 2: Today's News**
Discuss the concept of *sin*. There are three kinds of sin: Mortal sin destroys our relationship with God; serious Venial sin and less serious Venial sin weaken or take away from our relationship with God, but do not destroy it. Brainstorm with the children and list some of the evils happening in our world. The children may use words, phrases, or cartoons to depict incidents in the T.V. screens.

**Suggested Extra Project: Reconciliation Booklet**
Create a booklet (one for each child?). Prepare the children on how to examine their consciences. Use the ten Commandments as guidelines. If they wish, they can bring their booklet to the priest during Reconciliation.

**Note:** It is better for the student to mention one sin that he/she is truly sorry for, and try to tell why, rather than to list many sins that she or he does not even understand.

## The Eucharist

**Activity 1: Prepare for Mass**
If possible, take the children on a tour of the church. Point out the altar, candles, and Bible. Also show them the vestments, paten, and host.

**Extra Activity:**
This note can be done at home and brought to share at the next class. Read I Cor. 11:23–25, or have a student read it aloud.

**Activity 3: The Eucharist Celebration**
Have the children learn the two large parts of the Mass: I Liturgy of the Word, and II Liturgy of the Eucharist.

**The Communion Rite: The Sacred Bread and Wine**
Continue explaining the Communion Rite. Before First Communion, take time out to practice the procedure with a wafer and juice until the students feel at ease. Even older children need to review procedure and be reminded to respond with "Amen" after the Eucharist Minister says "Body of Christ" and "Blood of Christ."

**The Closing Rites**
Concentrate on the children's input, not on their spelling, etc. Take time to listen to their responses and affirm their responses.

**Suggested Extra Project:**
Ask the children to make a Communion mini-banner for their home. The family can assist. When they are complete you may wish to display the banners in class for a time. **Directions:** Make a banner at home. Create your banner of construction paper first. Put a photograph of you on it. Then decorate it with other pictures and items that describe events in the Communion Rite.

## Confirmation

**Activity 2: A Request Letter and Bible Search**
Discuss the meaning of Confirmation. Talk about the outline of the letter requesting Confirmation. Allow any questions. Pass out notebook paper and have the student compose the first draft of the request letter.

When they finish with their first draft letter, have them do the Bible search. Enough Bibles should be available to allow children to work in small groups.

**Activity 3:**
Complete the Bible verse following the numbers. Discuss the meaning of *Pentecost*.

**Activity 4:**
Before instructing the children to color the stained-glass window, match the words with the definitions. Allow time for discussion and examples. Pray, "Come, Holy Spirit..."

**Activity 5:**
Have the children make fruit on the tree by circling the word with the shapes of fruit. Tell them that the fruit are the effects of the Gifts of the Holy Spirit, and shows our good actions. Share their Good Spirit incidents. Explain the necessity for a community to possess this Good Spirit.

## Matrimony

**Activity 1:**
Allow time for students to read Genesis I. Discuss God's love for all creatures, but especially for man and woman. You may wish to play instrumental background music while the children color. Have the children share their pictures with the class when everyone is finished.

**Activity 2:**
Use dotted lines for students to trace. If there is limited space, draw the jars only. Fill in the spaces from Jn. 2:1–11. Review the meaning of *Matrimony*. Stress that this is Jesus' First Miracle at the request of his mother. Matrimony is the foundation for families.

**Activity 3:**
Marriage is a sacrament between man and woman. The priest or deacon is the main witness, and the community the other witness. Be sensitive to students who are in single-parent families. Remind students that Vows are not a once in a lifetime experience; they have to be renewed often, and with marriage are challenging responsibilities.

**Activity 4:**
Remind the children that we begin now to prepare for the future. We grow in love and sacrifice with God's Grace and our effort to do good.

## Anointing of the Sick

**Activity 1:**
Adapt the drawing. Tell the children that *viaticum* means food for the journey. Ask the children if they have ever attended or helped at a Sacrament of Anointing Liturgy. Where was it? Who came? How did they celebrate? Did young people assist in any way?

**Activity 2:**
This is an informative page. Very few have attended an anointing of the sick, unless it was in their home with their family gathered to pray for the ailing person.

**Activity 3:**
In order to serve others we need to respect our own bodies. This page can be completed aloud as a group. After each correct answer, students can copy onto their own page. In the culture we are in, it is necessary to point out the ways of destroying our health.

**Suggested Extra Activity:**
Provide paper for students to make a poster. Glue it to cardboard to be hung on the walls, etc.

## Holy Orders

**Activity 1:**
Allow time for the students to complete the puzzle. When all are finished, read aloud and allow time for questions. Learn the Bible quote from Isaiah 61:1.

**Activity 2:**
Discover if the students can distinguish between priest, bishop, and deacon. Stress their own role in the sharing of the priesthood. It would be good to invite a priest in to speak about Holy Orders and why he chose to serve the people of God in this way.

**Acitvity 3:**
Find out if the students know the names of the Pope, pastor, priest, and deacons in their Parish. They are usually named in the bulletin. Have Bibles for research. If time allows, read aloud as a group.